OLYMPIC SPORTS

OLYMPIC BOXING

BY LUKE HANLON

SportsZone
An Imprint of Abdo Publishing
abdobooks.com

abdobooks.com

Published by Abdo Publishing, a division of ABDO, PO Box 398166, Minneapolis, Minnesota 55439.

Printed in the United States of America, North Mankato, Minnesota.
102024
012025

THIS BOOK CONTAINS RECYCLED MATERIALS

Cover Photo: USA Boxing USAB
Interior Photos: Scott Heavey/Getty Images Sport/Getty Images, 5; Ryan Garza/The Flint Journal/AP Images, 6; Patrick Semansky/AP Images, 8; Richard Lautens/Toronto Star/Getty Images, 9; Theo Wargo/Getty Images for Women's Sports Foundation/Getty Images Entertainment/Getty Images, 10; Smiley N. Pool/Houston Chronicle/Hearst Newspapers/Getty Images, 12; George Grantham Bain Collection/Library of Congress, 15; HUM Images/Universal Images Group/Getty Images, 16; Bill Sikes/AP Images, 19; Richard Pelham/Getty Images Sport/Getty Images, 20–21; Han Haidan/China News Service/Getty Images, 23; STF/AFP/Getty Images, 25; Allsport/Hulton Archive/Getty Images, 26; Bettmann/Getty Images, 29, 30; Michael Cooper/Getty Images Sport/Getty Images, 31; Focus On Sport/Getty Images Sport/Getty Images, 32; EPU/AFP/Getty Images, 35; Buda Mendes/Getty Images Sport/Getty Images, 38; Alberto Pizzoli/AFP/Getty Images, 41; Dean Mouhtaropoulos/Getty Images Sport/Getty Images, 42; Luis Robayo/AFP/Getty Images, 44

Editor: Haley Williams
Series Designer: Karli Kruse

Library of Congress Control Number: 2024938350

Publisher's Cataloging-in-Publication Data

Names: Hanlon, Luke, author.
Title: Olympic boxing / by Luke Hanlon
Description: Minneapolis, Minnesota: ABDO Publishing, 2025 | Series: Olympic sports | Includes online resources and index.
Identifiers: ISBN 9781098295486 (lib. bdg.) | ISBN 9798384916482 (ebook)
Subjects: LCSH: Olympic games--Juvenile literature. | Boxing--Juvenile literature. | Olympians (Olympic athletes)--Juvenile literature. | Olympics--History--Juvenile literature. | Sports--Juvenile literature.
Classification: DDC 796.83--dc2

TABLE OF CONTENTS

CHAPTER 1

ON THE VERGE OF HISTORY

Claressa Shields piled on pressure early. In the second round of the 2012 Olympic women's middleweight gold-medal bout, the American swarmed Nadezda Torlopova. While the Russian had a lot more experience, Shields had a youthful and energetic fighting style. Her combination of speed and aggressiveness overwhelmed Torlopova throughout the fight.

Women's boxing became a medal event at the Olympics for the first time in 2012. At 17 years old, Shields went to London, England, planning to bring home a historic first gold medal. She had control throughout most of the fight. As the clock ticked down in the fourth and final round, Shields held a comfortable lead. Her confidence grew as she dodged multiple punches thrown by Torlopova. With less than a minute to go in the round, Torlopova paused to regain energy. Shields decided to have a little fun with her opponent. She stuck out her

Claressa Shields, *right*, was one of only two American boxers to medal at the 2012 Olympics in London, England.

Friends and family cheered on Shields during the Olympics from her hometown of Flint, Michigan.

tongue to taunt Torlopova. The gold medal Shields had worked so hard for felt like it was within reach.

A MAN'S SPORT

Shields was born in Flint, Michigan, in 1995. By the time she was two years old, her father had been sent to prison. Without him around, her mother coped with alcohol. That meant Shields had to take care of herself and her siblings. Some days she didn't eat because there was not enough food in the house for everyone. Most nights she slept on the floor.

Shields's dad, Bo, was released from prison when she was nine. A former boxer himself, Bo took Shields to a gym so she could see the sport in action. Shields became obsessed with boxing right away and wanted to try it. Her temper had gotten her in trouble at school after she hit a bully. Since she could not hit other kids at school, Shields figured it would be better to do it in the ring. But Bo didn't think so. He told Shields that boxing was a man's sport and that she was too pretty to box.

Shields would not give in easily. She pleaded with other members of her family to get Bo to change his mind. After gaining the support of multiple family members, Shields had them all vote on whether she could box. The majority of the family voted yes, which convinced Bo to let Shields step into the ring. Once Shields started boxing, it took over her life. She began studying legends such as Joe Louis and Sugar Ray Robinson. Shields also spent most of her free time in the gym training.

In 2006, 11-year-old Shields started working with Jason Crutchfield. He was a former boxer that grew up near Flint. He saw potential in Shields right away. Crutchfield started coaching and training her for free. He also let Shields stay at his house when she did not have a place to stay.

The pair was still working together in 2009. That year, the International Olympic Committee (IOC) announced that

As a kid, Shields played basketball and ran track to help her train for boxing.

women's boxing would make its Olympic debut at the 2012 Games. Shields was only 14 when the decision became official. But Crutchfield was confident she would be ready by the time the Olympics took place.

Shields channeled her temper to develop into an aggressive fighter. She used her strength and speed to apply tons of pressure to her opponents. Growing up with short, skinny arms, Shields earned the nickname "T-Rex." It became a fitting description for her ferocious fighting style as well.

Shields's skills were on full display early in her amateur career. She brought an undefeated record into the US Olympic Boxing Team Trials in 2012. At the Trials, she competed in the middleweight division with other women who weighed no more than 75 kilograms (165 lbs). Shields was the youngest in the talented division. Despite facing former national and world champions, she won all four of her fights.

GOING FOR GOLD

One step remained for Shields to earn a spot in the London Games. Her performance at the US Olympic Trials earned her a spot in the 2012 World Championships. If she finished as one of the top two Americans in the competition, she would earn a

Amateur boxers either wear red or blue depending on which corner they are assigned to for the bout.

spot in the Olympics. In the quarterfinals, Shields battled with Great Britain's Savannah Marshall. While Shields felt she had won, the judges disagreed. It was the first loss of her career. However, the disappointment of losing did not last long. Marshall went on to win the tournament. That ranked Shields high enough for her to qualify for the Olympics.

Boxing experts did not give Shields much of a chance to win gold in London. Most did not expect the teenager to even

Shields, *right*, was inspired by boxer Laila Ali, *left*, who is the daughter of 1960 Olympian and former men's heavyweight champion Muhammad Ali.

make the podium. But Shields was determined to prove them wrong. Her first bout came against Sweden's Anna Laurell. After losing the first round, Shields came back to win in a narrow decision.

Shields seemed headed toward a rematch with Marshall. The British boxer came in as the favorite to win gold. She also had the support of her home country. However, Kazakhstan's Marina Volnova upset Marshall in the quarterfinals. Instead of her chance at revenge, Shields now had to fight Volnova. And Shields did not suffer the same fate as Marshall. She beat Volnova 29–15. After the fight, Volnova said she could not keep up with Shields's quick punches.

Many boxing fans had not heard of Shields before the Olympics. But she quickly developed a following in London. Fans were drawn to her fast-paced style. She threw punches early and often, which led to exciting bouts. Her enthusiasm and fighting style even drew comparisons to legendary boxer

THE FIRE INSIDE

Claressa Shields's journey to the gold medal in 2012 reminded people of the 1976 film *Rocky*. The movie is about an underdog boxer who fights for the world heavyweight title. Some producers in Hollywood thought Shields's story would also make a good movie. So did movie writer and director Barry Jenkins. He wrote a script about Shields's childhood and her run to the 2012 gold medal. The 2024 movie is called *The Fire Inside*.

Shields is declared the winner of the women's middleweight gold-medal bout after defeating Nadezda Torlopova, *left*, 19–12.

Muhammad Ali, who won light heavyweight gold at the 1960 Olympics in Rome, Italy.

During the gold-medal bout between Shields and Torlopova, the crowd quickly fell in love with Shields. Chants of "U-S-A!" started in the first round. Shields used her aggressiveness against former world champion Torlopova. Shields stayed in close range with the Russian. She wanted it to be a physical fight. After an even first round, Shields started taking over in the second. She landed a few hard punches to Torlopova's body. Then she delivered some vicious hooks. Like other fighters at the Games, Torlopova could not handle Shields's speed.

Shields won the second and third rounds. By the fourth round, she knew that gold was in her grasp. The crowd roared for Shields as the clock ran down at the end of the fourth round. After the bout, the referee raised Shields's hand in the air. She was declared the Olympic champion. All Shields could do was smile. She had achieved her goal of winning gold. Shields was the first women's Olympic middleweight boxing champion.

CHAPTER 2

ANCIENT HISTORY

The first modern Olympics were held in Athens, Greece, in 1896. However, the ancient Olympic Games began in Greece more than 1,000 years earlier. Boxing was a key part of the ancient Games. The sport made its debut in 688 BC. While Olympic boxing has drastically evolved since then, some of the basics of the sport have remained the same. Bouts were one-on-one contests with both fighters wearing gloves. Other fighting strategies such as wrestling or kicking were not allowed.

Despite its history in ancient Greece, boxing was not included in the first two modern Olympics. The sport made its debut in the modern Games in St. Louis in 1904. The boxing event featured 18 American boxers competing across seven weight classes. The sport stuck around for the 1908 Games in London. However, four years later, the sport was dropped from the Olympics. The host country, Sweden, thought boxing

At the 1904 Games in St. Louis, American Oliver Kirk became the only boxer to win gold medals in two different weight classes at the same Olympics.

Women's boxing was a display event at the 1904 Olympics, meaning no medals were awarded to the athletes who competed.

was too dangerous and decided to ban it. Boxing returned to the Olympics at the 1920 Games in Antwerp, Belgium. Then in 1924, the IOC voted to make boxing a mandatory sport at the Olympics.

Women began boxing in the 1720s. However, for more than 100 years, only men were allowed to box in the Olympics. Critics argued that there were not enough women boxers to include the sport in the Games. Others said boxing was too dangerous for women. Women's boxing finally made its Olympic debut at the 2012 Games. Three weight classes were featured that year. By the 2024 Olympics in Paris, France, there were six weight classes for women's boxing.

FAIR COMPETITION

Olympic boxing has always been divided into different weight classes. The weight classes are used to make sure bouts take place between athletes of a similar size. If a boxer is heavier than his or her opponent, it would give that boxer a big advantage.

The number of weight classes for Olympic boxing has changed many times throughout the years. The 2024 Games featured seven weight classes for men's boxing. The classes ranged from 51 kilograms (112 lbs) to more than 92 kilograms (203 lbs). The six weight classes in women's boxing ranged

ADDING BRONZES

In the early years of Olympic boxing, three medals were awarded per weight class. The two boxers who lost in the semifinals would face each other to win a bronze medal. However, the International Boxing Association (IBA) changed that before the 1952 Olympics in Helsinki, Finland. The organization thought boxers did not have enough time to recover before fighting for bronze. Since 1952, each weight class has awarded two bronze medals.

from 50 kilograms (110 lbs) to 75 kilograms (165 lbs).

Each weight class has its own tournament to determine a champion. The winner of a bout moves on to the next round, while the loser is eliminated. The last two boxers face off in the gold-medal bout.

SCORING CHANGES

Since the 1928 Olympics in Amsterdam, Netherlands, each bout has been made up of three rounds that each last three minutes. Five judges score the bouts to determine a winner. Today, judges consider many factors when scoring a fight. This includes the number of punches thrown, technique, and control of the ring. Having an odd number of judges and rounds ensures that there are no ties. Not all bouts are decided by judges, though. A boxer can win a fight at any point by knocking out his or her opponent.

The scoring system has seen many changes over time. Relying on the opinions of human judges to score bouts led

More than 330 athletes took part in the 1992 Olympic men's boxing tournament in Barcelona, Spain.

to some controversial decisions. And none was more infamous than the light middleweight gold-medal bout at the 1988 Games in Seoul, South Korea.

American Roy Jones Jr. put in a dominant performance during the bout against South Korea's Park Si-Hun. There was little doubt that Jones Jr. had earned a gold medal. But three of the five judges thought Park won the fight. When Park was announced the winner, even the home crowd in Seoul was upset with the decision.

After that, the scoring system was significantly changed in time for the 1992 Olympics in Barcelona, Spain. Judges still scored the fights. But instead of using multiple factors

to decide a winner, judges only tracked punches landed using computers. Many boxing fans and journalists heavily criticized the new scoring system. They felt there was more to a boxing match than just landing punches.

At the 2024 Games in Paris, around 250 athletes competed in Olympic boxing. About half of those athletes were women.

Some of the top boxers from both the United States and Mexico decided to avoid the Olympics altogether because of that scoring change. Up until that change, the United States had been the most successful country in Olympic boxing.

VAL BARKER TROPHY

Starting in 1948, the IBA began handing out the Val Barker Trophy. The award goes to the best technical boxer at each Olympics. Although Roy Jones Jr. did not win light heavyweight gold in 1988, the IBA still honored him with the Val Barker Trophy that year. He became the third boxer to ever win the award without winning a gold medal in the same Olympics.

It topped the medal table in seven different Olympics. But starting in 1992, Cuba took over as the top force in boxing. The Caribbean country won the most boxing medals at every Olympics from 1992 to 2004.

GOING PRO

Olympic boxing saw another major shift in 2016. Up until that point, only amateur boxers could compete in the Games. However, the International Boxing Association (IBA) allowed professional boxers to compete at the Olympics starting at the 2016 Games in Rio de Janeiro, Brazil.

With pros coming to the Olympics, the IBA changed its scoring system to more closely reflect professional boxing. Each round is scored on a 10-point scoring system. In that system, judges score rounds either 10–9 or 10–8. Whichever boxer they think wins the round receives 10 points. Then the loser receives either nine or eight points depending on how significantly the boxer lost the round. Judges can also award a 10–10 score if they think the round is even.

Li Qian of China, *left*, and Laura Price of Great Britain compete in the women's middleweight gold-medal bout at the Tokyo Olympics in 2021.

Most boxing fans preferred the new scoring system over counting punches. But many people involved in the sport did not like the decision to allow professionals to compete. They felt that experienced pros would come in and crush amateurs who were just starting their careers. However, only three professionals competed at the 2016 Olympics. That number rose to 43 for the Tokyo Japan, Games in 2021. Of those 43 boxers, though, only six had more than four professional fights before competing in the Games. The Olympics remains a tournament for up-and-coming boxers.

CHAPTER 3

EARLY STARS

The Olympic Games were cancelled in 1940 and 1944 because of World War II (1939–45). After a 12-year delay, the Games returned in 1948. They were held in London. That year, Olympic boxing fans had the privilege of watching Hungarian László Papp for the first time. A natural athlete, Papp grew up competing in soccer and track and field. He started boxing when he was 18. Papp knew right away that was his sport of choice.

By the 1948 Olympics, the 22-year-old Papp had built an impressive amateur career as a middleweight. The hard-hitting southpaw knocked out his first three opponents in the Games. He then faced Johnny Wright of Great Britain in the gold-medal bout. The home fans in London were fully behind Wright. But Papp outlasted the Brit to win gold.

After his time in the Olympics, László Papp became a professional boxer. He was undefeated during his pro career.

Great Britain's Dick McTaggart, *right*, throws a punch at Ghana's Edward Blay at the 1960 Olympics in Rome.

Papp remained an amateur boxer through 1956. He went on to defend his gold at the Olympics in 1952 and 1956. That made Papp the first boxer to win three Olympic gold medals.

While Papp ended his Olympic career in 1956, Dick McTaggart was just beginning his. The British lightweight cruised to the gold-medal bout in the 1956 Olympics in Melbourne, Australia. There he faced defending European champion Harry Kurschat of Germany. McTaggart used his elusive defensive skills to upset the German and claim gold. The Brit also received the Val Barker Trophy for his impressive display.

At age 21, McTaggart received multiple offers to turn pro after winning gold. Despite making a small wage as a laborer, McTaggart had no desire to become a professional boxer. He went on to compete in the next two Olympics, winning bronze at the 1960 Games.

Like McTaggart, Boris Lagutin also won bronze at the 1960 Olympics. The Soviet boxer would go on to put together arguably the best amateur career in his country's history. Lagutin returned to the 1964 Olympics in Tokyo and won gold in the light middleweight division. Then at the 1968 Games in Mexico City, Mexico, he defended his gold medal by a unanimous decision. Lagutin finished his Olympic career with three medals.

GOLDEN AGAIN

American Eddie Eagan won light heavyweight gold at the 1920 Olympics in Antwerp, Belgium. After failing to medal four years later, Eagan took a break from boxing and tried bobsled instead. Three weeks before the 1932 Winter Olympics in Lake Placid, New York, Eagan was added to the US four-man bobsled team. He helped the team win gold. Eagan is the only person to ever win a gold medal in both the Summer and Winter Olympics.

AMERICAN ICONS

The United States has a long history of success in Olympic boxing. No country has won more golds or overall medals. The United States has also produced some of the biggest stars the sport has ever seen.

If it wasn't for Floyd Patterson getting in trouble a lot as a kid, he might have never competed at the Olympics. Due to bad behavior, 10-year-old Patterson went to a boys' reform school in New York. That is where he was introduced to boxing. At 16, Patterson won an amateur middleweight title in New York. A year later, he was boxing against middleweights at the 1952 Olympics in Helsinki, Finland.

Patterson had incredibly quick hands. During bouts, he would hold his hands up high and close to his face to defend himself. Once he saw an opening to strike, his opponent was in trouble. Patterson won his opening four fights at the 1952 Games by knockout. The gold-medal bout was no different. He hit his opponent with a brutal uppercut and knocked him out 74 seconds into the first round.

Floyd Patterson, *left*, was one of five US men's boxers to win gold at the 1952 Olympics.

Few boxing fans had heard of Cassius Clay before the 1960 Olympics. And there was a chance most never would have. Clay had a great fear of flying. He almost refused to fly from his hometown of Louisville, Kentucky, to Rome for the Games. To make sure he got there safely, Clay bought a parachute and wore it during the flight.

Boxing fans were glad that Clay agreed to go to Rome. He quickly won over crowds with his fancy footwork. He had the ability to dodge punches with ease. Clay could also quickly land combinations that took down opponents. He mixed his entertaining fighting style with a charming personality.

The light heavyweight class in Rome had multiple medal winners from the 1956 Games. Clay easily beat two of them on his way to the gold medal. After the 1960 Games, Clay turned pro. Four years later, upon becoming world heavyweight champion, he changed his name to Muhammad Ali. Today, Ali remains one of the most famous athletes of all time.

George Foreman eventually established a rivalry with Ali as a fellow heavyweight contender. But before he turned pro,

Muhammad Ali, then known as Cassius Clay, was 18 years old when he won light heavyweight gold at the 1960 Olympics.

Muhammad Ali carried the Olympic torch and lit the cauldron at the 1996 Games in Atlanta, Georgia.

Foreman started his amateur career in California. Foreman had only fought in 20 matches when he went to Mexico City for the 1968 Olympics.

While Foreman lacked experience, he did not lack size. The 6-foot-3, 218-pound heavyweight possessed immense strength. Relying on a powerful left jab, Foreman knocked out two of his three opponents before reaching the gold-medal bout. That match was no different. Foreman battered the Soviet Union's Jonas Čepulis. In the second round, the referee stopped the fight and declared Foreman the gold medalist.

The 1976 US Olympic boxing team had no shortage of talent. Regarded as one of the best amateur teams in history,

Sugar Ray Leonard, *right*, was inducted into the International Boxing Hall of Fame in 1997.

the US men won five gold medals that year in Montreal, Canada. The team featured brothers and future pro champions Leon and Michael Spinks. Howard Davis Jr., the 1976 Val Barker Trophy winner, was also on the team. However, none of those boxers was a bigger star than "Sugar" Ray Leonard.

READY FOR THE OPPORTUNITIES

Heavyweight Joe Frazier made it to the finals of the US Olympic Trials ahead of the 1964 Games. But he lost to fellow American Buster Mathis. While Frazier did not make the Olympic team, he traveled to Tokyo as an alternate. However, when Mathis broke a knuckle during training, Frazier replaced him. Frazier went on to be the only American boxer to win gold at the 1964 Olympics.

Leonard said he was always drawn to boxing. His natural ability was on full display in Montreal. Leonard used his quickness to fool opponents. He would fake punches to get them to react to something that was not coming. That opened easy opportunities for Leonard to land big shots.

Leonard won his first five bouts in 1976 by unanimous decisions. That set up a light welterweight gold-medal bout against Cuba's Andres Aldama. Aldama had won all five of his fights by knockout. But his strength could not match Leonard's lighting quick hands and feet. As in all Leonard's previous bouts, every judge agreed Leonard deserved to win.

CHAPTER 4

CUBA TAKES OVER

With the introduction of a new scoring system at the 1992 Games, Cuba took over Olympic boxing. A big reason why was Cuban-style boxing emphasized hitting and dodging. While the country had its most success in the 1990s and early 2000s, it had a couple legendary boxers pave the way.

CUBAN LEGENDS

Teófilo Stevenson was 16 when he watched the 1968 Olympics. He saw Cuban boxers Enrique Regüeiferos and Rolando Garbey each win silver medals. Those were the first medals Cuba had ever won in Olympic boxing. Their wins inspired Stevenson to strive for Olympic glory himself.

Four years later, Stevenson made his Olympic debut in Munich, West Germany. The bruising heavyweight reached the gold-medal bout by knocking out all his opponents. West Germany's Peter Hussing lost to Stevenson in the semifinals.

Teófilo Stevenson, *left*, defeated Soviet Pyotr Zayev in the heavyweight gold-medal bout at the 1980 Games in Moscow, Russia.

GOLDEN BOY

American Oscar De La Hoya was born to be a boxer. His grandfather was an amateur boxer in Mexico, and his dad, Joel, was a pro boxer there. De La Hoya began boxing at the age of four. He then went on to represent Team USA at the 1992 Olympics at 19 years old. Two years before those Games, De La Hoya promised his dying mother he would become an Olympic champion. And he did just that. De La Hoya earned the nickname "Golden Boy" after taking home the lightweight gold medal.

Hussing said he had never been hit as hard as when Stevenson knocked him out. Stevenson then won gold without even fighting. His opponent had to forfeit due to an injury. Despite not having a gold-medal bout, Stevenson received the Val Barker Trophy for his powerful knockouts.

Stevenson came back even stronger for the 1976 Games. The Cuban knocked out his first three opponents in less than eight total minutes of ring time. Then he won gold after his opponent's trainer stopped the gold-medal bout in the third round. Stevenson defended his heavyweight title again at the 1980 Olympics in Moscow, Russia. He became the first boxer to win three golds in the same weight class.

Just as he was inspired by previous Cuban fighters, Stevenson helped establish Cuba as a powerhouse in Olympic boxing. However, the country boycotted the 1984 Olympics in Los Angeles, California, and the 1988 Olympics in Seoul, South Korea. This was due to Cuba's government following the political system of communism. The country feared that its athletes would not be safe in the United States or South Korea, as both countries were against communism.

Once Cuba returned to the Olympics in 1992, its boxing team was set up for a golden era led by Félix Savón. Savón had already established himself as one of the best boxers in the world by the 1992 Olympics. He had won three amateur world titles by then. He would have been favored to win gold in 1988 if Cuba had participated in the Olympics. Even so, Savón made up for the lost time. He tortured his competitors with powerful punches and smooth footwork. He could avoid punches just as easily as he could land them. In his final two bouts at the 1992 Games, he outscored his opponents 37–4 to win gold.

Savón remained committed to representing Cuba at the Olympics. Despite offers to turn pro, he fought in two more Games. In 2000, he joined Stevenson and László Papp as the only boxers to ever win three gold medals.

A NEW ERA

Cuba's dominance in Olympic boxing began to fade in 2008. But the country still produced great talent. That year, Roniel Iglesias made his Olympic debut at the Games in Beijing, China. He took home a bronze. Four years later in London, Iglesias won light welterweight gold.

Andy Cruz was one of five Cuban boxers to medal at the Tokyo Olympics in 2021. He won gold in the men's lightweight final.

Iglesias returned to the Olympics in 2016 in Rio de Janeiro. However, he lost before the semifinals. When the Tokyo Olympics in 2021 came around, Iglesias was 32. Many people doubted that he could compete with the field of younger boxers in their prime. Iglesias silenced any of those doubts by beating Great Britain's Pat McCormack in a unanimous decision to win another Olympic gold. The win made Iglesias one of 10 boxers to win three Olympic medals.

Cuba continued to showcase its boxing skills at the 2024 Olympics. Arlen López came into Paris having won golds in both Rio and Tokyo. Competing in the middleweight division, López won his first two bouts to set up a semifinal matchup against Oleksandr Khyzhniak of Ukraine. The boxers exchanged blows in an epic bout. While Khyzhniak won by a split decision, López earned a bronze to take home his third Olympic medal.

A NEW BOXING POWER

Uzbekistan burst onto the international boxing scene at the 2016 Olympics. In Rio, Uzbekistan won three golds and seven total medals in the sport. Then at the Tokyo Olympics in 2021, Bakhodir Jalolov was the country's only boxer to medal. When he defended his gold at the 2024 Games, he clinched Uzbekistan's fifth boxing gold of those Olympics.

A new Cuban talent emerged at the 2024 Games as well. Erislandy Alvarez won three unanimous decisions to cruise to the lightweight gold-medal bout. He faced France's Sofiane Oumiha in front of a rowdy crowd in Paris. The massive cheers died down as Alvarez took control of the fight to win gold. His title extended Cuba's streak of winning at least one boxing gold at every Olympics since 2012.

CHAPTER 5

WOMEN IN THE RING

As soon as women's boxing became an Olympic sport in 2012, many talented boxers emerged as stars. Katie Taylor was already well known in her home country of Ireland before those Games. Her country chose her as flag bearer at the opening ceremony in London.

After winning her first two fights, Taylor faced off against Sofya Ochigava of Russia in the lightweight gold-medal bout. A large section of traveling Irish fans roared as Taylor entered the arena. They kept the noise up throughout the match as Taylor battled with Ochigava. In a back-and-forth fight, Taylor landed one big hook in the second round that proved to be the difference. The judges scored the fight 10–8 in favor of Taylor. The crowd erupted to celebrate Ireland's only gold medal at the 2012 Olympics. Taylor quickly became a superstar across the world of boxing.

Katie Taylor was taught how to box by her father, who was a former fighter, when she was 12 years old.

Nicola Adams holds up her gold medal after winning the women's flyweight final at the 2016 Olympics.

Taylor was not the only fan favorite at the London Games. Great Britain's Nicola Adams fought all her bouts in front of a home crowd. Each time, the rowdy fans helped bring the best out of the charismatic flyweight.

Adams had her toughest test in the gold-medal bout as she faced Chinese boxer Ren Cancan. Cancan had previously won three world championships. But she was no match for Adams. The Brit landed multiple devastating blows in the second round that sent Cancan to the mat. Adams went on to win the first flyweight gold in Olympic women's boxing history.

Adams came into the 2016 Olympics as a favorite to win gold again. But this time, she would have to do it without the support of a home crowd. That proved to be no issue for Adams. She won all three of her bouts by unanimous decision to defend her flyweight gold.

FIGHTING FOR GOLD

Claressa Shields stormed onto the scene in London to win middleweight gold at 17 years old. Shields's run to gold stunned boxing fans. But the American prodigy only got better after the 2012 Games.

Four years after Shields won gold, she entered the 2016 Games with much different expectations set for her. The feisty middleweight had not lost a fight since before the 2012 Games. She had also claimed multiple world championships during that time. Instead of shocking the boxing world, Shields needed to affirm her status as the favorite in the tournament. And she did just that. Shields won all three of her fights by a unanimous decision. With her gold in Rio, Shields

FIGHT LIKE A FROG

While training for the Tokyo Olympics, Sena Irie had times when she wanted to quit boxing. One thing that kept her going was looking at pictures of frogs, which are her favorite animal. Irie even named her fighting strategy at the Games "operation aggressive horned frog." Channeling frogs worked wonders for Irie. She won featherweight gold at the Tokyo Games in 2021. Irie became the first Japanese woman to win an Olympic boxing medal.

became the first American to win back-to-back Olympic boxing gold medals. In addition to winning gold, Shields was awarded the first women's Val Barker Trophy.

In 2015, 17-year-old Busenaz Sürmeneli met the president of Turkey and promised him that she would win an Olympic medal one day. At the Tokyo Olympics in 2021, she had a chance to make that promise a reality. Fighting in the women's welterweight division, Sürmeneli possessed bruising power. She used it to pummel her opponents. In Sürmeneli's first

Busenaz Sürmeneli, *left*, secured one of Turkey's two Olympic gold medals at the Tokyo Games in 2021.

three bouts, she won every single round. That set up a gold-medal bout against China's Gu Hong.

Gu proved to be a tough opponent. After losing the first round, Sürmeneli landed several powerful hooks near the end of the second. And in the final round, Sürmeneli was able to finish strong and claim gold. It was the first Olympic boxing gold medal in Turkey's history.

A 34-year-old Li Qian from China entered the ring at the 2024 Games having boxed for half her life. When she made her Olympic debut eight years prior in Rio, she took home bronze in the middleweight division. Then she made the gold-medal bout in Tokyo. But she lost in a unanimous decision against Great Britain's Lauren Price to settle for silver.

After Tokyo, Li said she regretted the loss to Price. So Li entered Paris determined to win gold. She easily won her first three bouts to reach the middleweight final. Then she won a 4–1 decision to secure gold. With that win, Li became the first woman boxer to medal in three consecutive Olympics.

HISTORIC WEIGHT CLASS

Li Qian wasn't the only boxer to make history in her weight class at the 2024 Olympics. She faced Atheyna Bylon in the women's middleweight gold-medal bout. By winning silver, Bylon became the first woman from Panama to ever win an Olympic medal. Meanwhile, Cindy Ngamba earned a bronze after losing to Bylon in the semifinals. That secured the first medal for the Refugee Olympic Team.

GLOSSARY

amateur
A person who plays a sport without getting paid.

bout
A boxing fight.

boycotted
Refused to take part in an event as a form of protest.

combinations
Multiple punches landed in a row.

debut
First appearance.

forfeit
An automatic loss.

hooks
Punches thrown with a boxer's elbow bent.

infamous
Known for having a bad reputation.

jabs
Straightforward punches.

knockout
A conclusion of a fight in which one competitor is physically unable to continue.

prodigy
A young player who has a great natural ability for a sport.

professional
A person who gets paid to perform.

rivalry
A fierce and ongoing competition between two opponents.

southpaw
A left-handed boxer.

taunt
To provoke someone with insulting words or actions.

unanimous decision
When every judge agrees that a fighter won a bout.

uppercut
A punch delivered in an upward motion.

MORE INFORMATION

BOOKS

McDougall, Chrös. *The Olympics Encyclopedia*. Abdo, 2022.

Olson, Ethan. *Muhammad Ali: Boxing Legend*. Press Room Editions, 2024.

Price, Karen. *GOATs of Olympic Sports*. Abdo, 2022.

ONLINE RESOURCES

Booklinks
NONFICTION NETWORK
FREE! ONLINE NONFICTION RESOURCES

To learn more about Olympic boxing, please visit **abdobooklinks.com** or scan this QR code. These links are routinely monitored and updated to provide the most current information available.

INDEX

ABOUT THE AUTHOR

Luke Hanlon is a sportswriter and editor who lives in Minneapolis, Minnesota. He's covered multiple Olympic sports for TeamUSA.com.